THE LAST COAT

JOSEPH'S JOURNEY TO THE PALACE

JAMES TAWIAH MENSAH

Published by GloriPub
©Copyright 2018 James Tawiah Mensah
Unless otherwise stated, all Scripture quotations are taken from the Holy Bible, New International Version (NIV) Full Life Study Bible. Copyright 1985, 1995, 2002 by Zondervan Publishing House.
ISBN-10: 0997621389
ISBN-13: 978-0-9976213-8-9

Also by James Tawiah Mensah

SUCCESS: WHAT IS IT ALL ABOUT?

GIVING: WHAT IS IT ALL ABOUT?

LOYALTY: WHAT IS IT ALL ABOUT?

THE WORD OF GOD v. THE WORK OF GOD

Contents

Dedication   i

Acknowledgement   v

Foreword   vii

Introduction   xi

THE FIRST COAT   1

THE SECOND COAT   15

THE THIRD COAT   33

THE LAST COAT   43

MY THOUGHT   59

Conclusion   73

Dedication

To My Family

TO GOD BE THE GLORY

Acknowledgement

My late parents, Mr. Abednego Aklama Mensah and Mad. Christiana Charkuor Charway, whose words of wisdom and character shaped mine; my brothers, Rev. Michael Martey Mensah, Ghana and Nigeria; Mr. James Martey Mensah, Mr. William Mensah and sisters; late Ms. Adelaide Adoley Mensah, Ms. Belinda Marteykuor Mensah, Ms. Ruth Akweley Mensah, Ms. Letitia Agoyo Mensah and Ms. Alberta Abah Mensah, all in Ghana, whose contributions, in various times and ways, also helped to make me what I am today.

Rev. Benjamin Kwadjo Boakye, Senior Pastor, Ebenezer Assembly of God Church, Bronx, New York, USA, my present pastor, made me the Superintendent, Sunday School Department, and provided the tools needed to succced. Rev. Emmanuel Yawson. My good buddies, Brother George Kwame Arkhurst and Minister Tony Aghamiogie and fellow Sunday School teachers, encouraged me in diverse ways.

Also, the students who listen to me every Sunday inspired me with their contributions in class. All Department leaders and entire members of Ebenezer Assembly of God

Church, Bronx, New York, USA, gave me the opportunity to use my talent and gift to serve; Mr. Awuku Darko, Armor-bearer, Living Faith Ministry Int., Mount Vernon, New York, USA, and his wife, Sister Unity Agyeman, stood by me during the writing with words of encouragement. Mr. and Mrs. Isaac and Judith Amoah, Bronx, New York, USA; Mr. and Mrs. Raymond and Abigail Kotei, West Haven, Connecticut, USA, my biggest fans; Mr. Joseph Nartey, my brother-in-law, Bronx, New York, USA; a very, very good friend, Pastor Isaac Twumasi, Ghana; Mr. Patrick Lucas Onasis Aryerh, Ghana, (aka P.L.O Aryerh); Mrs. Anna Christa Rawls Sackey, edited and wrote the foreword for "Success: What is it all about?" Rev. William Kanych, Senior Pastor, Faith Assembly of God, Yonkers, New York, USA, edited and wrote the foreword for "Giving: What is it all about?" Rev. Nancy Pierre, edited and wrote the foreword for "Loyalty: What is it all about?" Pastor Kwame Acheampong, author, "Fashion and Faith," and Ms. Joyce Ohene-Amoah, author, "Building A Healthy Lasting Marriage," inspired me.

Foreword

On the 6th of December 2015, I was on an unannounced visit to Ebenezer Assembly of God's Sunday service to worship with my beloved brother in Christ, Rev. Benjamin Boakye. It happened that Minister James Mensah was the preacher of the day. He was introduced to the pulpit with much applause and standing ovation from the congregation. I immediately felt this brother might be a great preacher. Then he introduced his theme: "THE LAST COAT." I TRULY WEPT DURING THE PREACHING OF HIS MESSAGE. It was a thrilling and soul-stirring and mind-cultivating message that gave me hope and a sense of direction.

Many have written their versions about Joseph's character; many have expressed their views about his personality, but another piece was revealed that day. A preacher once said, "The coat of many colors meant confusion but in the midst of his confusion, there was an arrow of contempt shot at him." Different perspective altogether, if you'd agree. What makes this book worthwhile? What makes this book a must-read?

The writer's choice of words relating to this remarkable character (Joseph) will be of much interest to you. His personality portrayed an epitome worthy of emulation. It is extremely difficult to attract a father's love among many brothers. Men of Joseph's kind around the world are facing the same dilemma of identity. Because of the cloud of envies and oppositions around them, they are struggling to discover who they really are and where they stand in their own family, the community and the world at large. The confusion over the beauty of this coat of many colors and the dreams of Joseph manifested themselves in a variety of ways.

This book, "THE LAST COAT," by Minister James Mensah, will help you expand and extend your vision beyond the schemes and techniques of giants that pose threats to your progress in life, marriage, relationship and financial breakthrough. Giant posts on your way to block your vision not to focus on what God plans for your life, but to force you to lose hope in yourself. It will also assist you to update your walk with Lord and add more faith and hope to your life as you go through everyday challenges. It has a lot of nuggets that shall blow up your mine. As you continue reading, scales would be removed from your eyes. You will regain your authority and take over full control of your life. With hope and long suffering, you will step into your greatness. I, therefore, highly recommend this profound book to you. May God richly bless you.

Reverend Eli Nutifafa,
Head Pastor and the Founder,
Global Winners Tabernacle,
Bronx, New York, USA

Introduction

"The righteous person may have many troubles, but the Lord delivers him from them all; he protects all his bones, not one of them will be broken" (Psalm 34:19, 20).

We met just a few weeks prior. And we had barely known each other. But there was this invincible admiration undergirding our relationship that attracted us to each other. I believe his love for the Lord, and that of mine, being the common thread running through us, was the underlining denominator. Therefore, I was not so much surprised when he showed up in front of our door that afternoon. I received and honored him with courtesy. The courtesy of ushering him in without any delay. He responded and followed me. Then I pointed him to one of the two seats we left at the back porch for our visitors. He accepted the gesture with a broad smile spreading across his face as he pulled the chair back to make room for his long legs.

He sat directly across from me. In front of us were two bottles of Fanta, with a plate of cookies in between. After exchanging pleasantries, we sank into a deep conversation. As I sipped mine, I urged him on to do same, but he reluctantly did. Somehow his reluctance persisted to my surprise. I never suspected anything eating him up emotionally ever since he entered my abode. His humble demeanor never revealed anything otherwise. His posture was of good standing and of absolute admiration. This posture effectively displayed his gentlemanly attitude. He composed and comported himself well like any visitor would do for a host. As we settled to discuss a few issues, there was this uninvited silence that interfered with our conversation. Then I lifted my eyes up to his at this moment to check what might have caused this silence. There I saw his eyes moistened and welled up with tears. I was taken aback. I immediately enquired of the reasons behind those tears. Pausing unapologetically, he took a deep breath. He, there and then, followed up by opening to me with his worries. While he narrated his story, tears unable to control rolled down his bony cheeks. He correspondingly wiped them with the back of his left hand. These sacred tears underlined the pain etched on his heart all along. He accumulated this pain little by little over the years and it had hardened like a sedimentary rock. The slowness with which he pronounced the words to describe the things he went through in the hands of his siblings, spoke more volume than the words themselves could articulate. The pain, culminating from the rejection and refusal, the marginalization and ostracization of his person, could clearly and visibly be seen behind every word he churned. His siblings, who were supposed to stand and show support in time of any tragedy, had instead ganged up against him. This unfortunate incident erected an invisible wall between them and himself, resulting in each group secluded and confined to its own corner. And though he felt hopeless and vulnerable as he sat in front of me, he mustered the needed courage to pour his heart out to me that fateful afternoon. He ascertained the truth pertaining to his ordeal by supplying dates and times with utmost precision. As concerned as I am for such issues, I sat there and listened to him with rapt attention and I was absolutely stunned by the sadness surrounding the whole episode. I sympathized with him and offered the solace he needed at the time to the best of my ability.

Family conflicts, or sibling rivalries to be precise, have been in existence for as long as man had lived on this earth. And it will never end anytime soon until the last man exits this earth. Man's inability to see others the way he sees himself is the cause of all these squabbles. We are so much consumed by pride and prejudice that we do not see any worth in others. We have become egocentric and selfish in our world of today. It is for these reasons, Paul advised us to

> *Do nothing out of selfish ambition or vain conceit. Rather, in humility value others above yourselves, not looking to*

your own interests but each of you to the interests of the others (Philippians 2:3, 4).

If we would only yield to this admonition, we would be able to keep a curb on these senseless conflicts.

All these conflicts started in the Garden of Eden when Adam pointed his fingers at Eve as the cause of their predicament: the eating of the forbidden fruit from the tree of the knowledge of good and evil. When Adam accused God for bringing in a woman he never asked Him for (Genesis 3:6-12). Cain killed Abel when his offering was rejected because of its poor quality (Genesis 2:8). Jacob fled to Laban when the mother conspired with him to trick the father as him being Esau. When Esau realized Jacob's deception and threatened to take his life, a sibling rivalry ensued as a result (Genesis 27:42-45). I was not surprised at all, not shocked, when my friend told his story to me. Sibling rivalry is nothing new, but the context, or the cause of the feud is what sets one issue apart from the other. If these feuds are not immediately curtailed, they take dimensions that are difficult to control. In Joseph's case, what he suffered in the hands of his brothers within the context of his age, the absence of his mother and the father's old age, raises more questions than could meet the eye.

The lessons Joseph learned and the experiences gained during his journey helped to make him what he became so he could live up to expectations. And yes, he did meet expectations when he left his Papa's house, when he served in Potiphar's house, when he oversaw the prisoners behind the Prison walls and when he managed the affairs of the nation in Pharaoh's palace. 'Life is not fair,' some are fond of saying. Yet, no matter how one is assaulted by events of life one has no control over, these tragic events come together to build one up for achievement of a goal. And Joseph was no exception. He had a fair share of life's onslaught and it built him. As we delve into the events of his coats changing, and therefore his rise to prominence and fame - a journey that defied all odds and thrust him to a vital position in a foreign land - we will pick up the lessons from the knowledge he acquired along the way. Let's pause to consider the following questions.

- How did it all start?
- Why couldn't his brothers consider his age and just disregard picking any altercation with him?
- Why couldn't they brush his attitude aside as childish and display of immaturity?
- Why didn't the merchants consider his youthful age and reject the transaction altogether?
- Why couldn't Potiphar believe him once more and prevent him from going to prison?

We will attempt to provide answers to these questions and others that might confront us. We will also consider the initial pointer that triggered the plot. The plot to assassinate him but for the timely arrival of the Ishmaelite merchants. The Teacher puts it in a better perspective saying, "A person's steps are directed by the Lord. How then can anyone understand their own way?" (Proverbs 20:24).

James Tawiah Mensah

Chapter One

THE FIRST COAT

"I have told you these things, so that in me you may have peace. In this world, you will have trouble. But take heart! I have overcome the world" (John 16:33)

His fame spread beyond parameters he could never have ever imagined. Under no circumstance, in his wildest dream did he think he could be so powerful and famous. He never perceived his renown soaring beyond bounds. That his assistance would be sought to lead the very people who rejected, refused, marginalized and abandoned him in the time he needed them the most. That his contribution to the liberation of his people from the tyranny of their enemies would be significant or magnificent. Considering his background - with regards to his birth - he was a 'nobody' in the eyes of the family members and of the society. But Jephthah defied all odds, scaled over all obstacles on his way and rose to the pinnacle of life. He became so powerful a warrior that life could not hide him anymore. That was God and Jephthah at work to bring a talent to the fore.

He was born out of wedlock and among step-brothers. It was no fault of his to have been born from the womb of a prostitute. Such misfortune was an albatross it initiated his rejection. The relationship between him and his siblings was cordial to the admiration of the town's folks when they were young. Jephthah enjoyed the company of his siblings. There was no sign of rivalry under any circumstance. They shared almost everything in common like it is usually seen among siblings. Their youthful exuberance was always at the fore in whatever they did. None claimed to be superior to the others. For they saw themselves as children of the same father. But as they grew older, cracks in their relationship began to emerge. The circumstance of his birth surfaced. This revelation set a foundation upon which the other children would begin to despise him. The children of the other woman put their heads together and decided to send him away so he would not be part in the share of the inheritance.

> *When they were grown up, they drove Jephthah away. "You are not going to get any inheritance in our family," they said, "because you are the son of another woman (Judges 11:2).*

Jephthah could not fathom such a cruel decision being taken against him by folks he knew as brothers. With pain deeply etched on his heart, "Jephthah fled from his brothers and settled in the land of Tob, where a gang of scoundrels gathered around him and followed him" (Judges 11:3). Jephthah's brothers thought their decision would be in their best interest, but little did they know there is a higher power that controls the affairs of man. The Bible puts it this way; "A person may think their own ways are right, but the Lord weighs the heart" (Proverbs 21:2).

Just as Jephthah was driven out by his siblings against his will, so was Joseph 'driven' into slavery by his brothers against his.

(A) The Giving of the First Coat (Gen. 37:3)

After Jacob's mother conspired with him to deceive the father, he fled to Laban, a relative of his mother's. There he fell in love with Laban's younger daughter, whom "I'll work for you seven years in return for your younger daughter Rachel" (Genesis 29:18). Laban readily agreed to Jacob's suggestion. For the next seven years he worked as the dowry for his daughter. But when the years were due, and the uncle refused to deliver his end of the bargain, Jacob demanded to know the reason behind the refusal,

> *Laban replied, "It is not our custom here to give the younger daughter in marriage before the older one. Finish this daughter's bridal week; then we will give you the younger one also, in return for another seven years of work" (Genesis 29:26, 27).*

Customs of the time wouldn't permit a younger daughter to be married away before the older. Leah, being the older was given to Jacob but he did not love her so he decided to work for another seven years for Rachel. The Bible says for the love he had for Rachel, the seven years passed in no time. He took his two wives, each with her servant and went home to his parents. Jacob extended so much love to Rachel that Leah was utterly neglected. So "When the Lord saw that Leah was not loved, he enabled her to conceive, but Rachel remained childless" (Genesis 29:31). Like Hannah, who was made fun of by her rivals, I believe so was with Rachel. The Bible described Hannah's situation thus;

> *Because the Lord had closed Hannah's womb, her rival kept provoking her in order to irritate her. This went on year after year. Whenever Hannah went up to the house of the Lord, her rival provoked her till she wept and would not eat. Her husband Elkanah would say to her, "Hannah, why are you weeping? Why don't you eat? Why are you downhearted? Don't I mean more to you than ten sons? (1 Samuel 1:6-8).*

Leah gave birth to four boys, at the time, Rachel had none. So, she decided to give her servant to her husband so the child that would come as result will wipe away her tears, the tears for what she claimed to be shameful among her peers. Her servant indeed gave birth to two sons, whom she named Dan and Naphtali. When the Lord opened Rachel's womb to give birth, she had a son and named him

Joseph. She had another son, Benjamin, but Rachel died while giving birth to him. So, "Now Israel loved Joseph more than any of his other sons, because he had been born to him in his old age; and he made an ornate robe for him" (Genesis 37:3). This coat of many colors distinguished Joseph from his peers. The pride with which he wore the coat always displayed his youthful exuberance. He was admired and adored by his younger brother Benjamin, who looked up to him for direction and counseling. This coat, given to Joseph by his father, was not just any coat but one that would mark the beginning of a journey that will turn his life in a direction never imagined.

The brothers saw the coat as a threat to their superiority. They hated him and would not treat him well. Whenever they interacted with him, they did it with malice and contempt. Joseph was too young to read meaning into their mean attitude and the cold shoulder they always gave him. Joseph went about his duties without the slightest suspicion until one day the father decided to send him after his brothers who had gone to graze the flocks. Without any hesitation, he readily obeyed his father and went on to perform the task the father gave him. Joseph never perceived anything sinister was awaiting him.

- What was the fate awaiting him as he approached his brothers?

- What decision did they take before he arrived in their presence? How did they plan to carry it out?
- Will they succeed in carrying it out?

The next segment will provide the answers as Joseph's story unfolds.

(B) The Stripping of the First Coat (Gen. 37:23)

Whenever Joseph went out with his brothers to graze the flock, he brought home bad report about their deeds. For this reason, they begrudged him with all intensity. With the coat the father made for him, the brothers saw it as a threat to their seniority. This did not sit well with them. What compounded the hatred was when he had the first dream and made it known. The announcement of same changed the dynamics of their relationship with him drastically. The Bible describes it thus:

> *Joseph had a dream, and when he told it to his brothers, they hated him all the more. He said to them, "Listen to this dream I had: We were binding sheaves of grain out in the field when suddenly my sheaf rose and stood upright, while your sheaves gathered around mine and bowed down to it." His brothers said to him, "Do you intend to reign over us? Will you actually rule us?" And they hated him all the more because of his dream and what he had said (Genesis 37:5-8).*

Joseph's dream was self-explanatory his brothers understood it. They did not need anyone to interpret the dream to them. It was clear and straight to the point but they were not prepared for a second dream. Neither were their parents. Whatever the Lord had destined you to be, will manifest definitely in due time. It wasn't long when God gave Joseph the second dream to confirm what He intended his destiny to be. Joseph's destiny was sealed and secured, and no one can change the purpose of God. While they sat around the fire telling folk stories, they were contemplating the first dream when

> *He told it to his brothers. "Listen," he said, "I had another dream, and this time the sun and moon and eleven stars were bowing down to me." When he told his father as well as his brothers, his father rebuked him and said, "What is this dream you had? Will your mother and I and your brothers actually come and bow down to the ground before you?" His brothers were jealous of him, but his father kept the matter in mind (Genesis 37:9-11).*

Yes, they hated him the more. This hatred set in motion this dangerous phenomenon of sibling rivalry. There and then, they began to orchestrate ways and means to eliminate him so his dreams would not come to pass. They wanted to defeat God's plan for Joseph. With all these schemes set in motion, little did they know their "heart is in the hand of the LORD; he directs it like a watercourse wherever he pleases" (Proverbs 21:1). From Joseph's quarters, there was nothing to indicate that his brothers were plotting to eliminate him. It never ever crossed his young mind. He never gave such heinous crime a thought. Joseph knew them to be his brothers, so when the father called him to follow them he took it as the usual outings with them. While he stood in front of his father,

> Israel said to Joseph, "As you know, your brothers are grazing the flocks near Shechem. Come, I am going to send you to them." "Very well," he replied. So, he said to him, "Go and see if all is well with your brothers and with the flocks, and bring word back to me." Then he sent him off from the Valley of Hebron... (Genesis 37:13, 14).

When Joseph was leaving the presence of his father, Jacob, nothing informed him that it would be the last time he would see him for many years to come. Neither did it occur to the father he was bidding his son the last goodbye for more than thirteen years to come. But it must happen, and it did. Then Joseph bowed his head down to the father and left his presence. He was wearing his admired coat of many colors. He went to his brother, Benjamin and told him the journey he was embarking on. "Dad had sent me to go and check on our elder brothers. And I am coming back in few days or hours depending how it goes," he confidently promised. He assured him he would brief him on all that would take place in the journey. No one ever fathomed it to be a journey of no return; a journey that was to change the course of his life, and of course, theirs too. A journey that would bring evil nurtured in the hearts of his blood brothers over the years to fruition. The execution of a wicked plot hatched over a long period of time. Jesus warned the disciples with these words, and same goes to us:

> *If they persecuted me, they will persecute you also. If they obeyed my teaching, they will obey yours also. They will treat you this way because of my name, for they do not know the one who sent me (John 15:20, 21).*

Joseph climbed hills and descended valleys as he headed towards Shechem. He perspired under the scorching afternoon sun of the Palestinian plains, while dust deposited on his tiny feet. He was talking to himself as to how he would frame the message the father asked him to deliver. He was excited to perform such a task for him. He greeted everyone he met as if he was obligated to do so. But did so out of courtesy and respect his father had passed on to him. In fact, this feat he had achieved told him he had come of age. It showed the boldness he possessed. He would able to stand on his own two feet to handle the flock should he be allowed. When he had arrived in Shechem, he could not trace the brothers' whereabouts so he wandered around asking those he met the whereabouts of ten men grazing flocks.

> *A man found him wandering around in the field and asked him, "What are you looking for?" He replied, "I'm looking for my brothers. Can you tell me where they are grazing their flocks?" "They have moved on from here," the man answered. "I heard them say, 'Let's go to Dothan.'* (Genesis 37: 15-17a)

Turning around and heading towards the direction the man pointed to him, "… Joseph went after his brothers and found them near Dothan" (Genesis 37:17b). But before he could set his eyes on the brothers as he descended the fourth or fifth hills, they saw him in a distance. And before he could reach them, they had agreed to eliminate him. They said,

> *"Here comes that dreamer!" they said to each other. "Come now, let's kill him and throw him into one of these cisterns and say that a ferocious animal devoured him. Then we'll see what comes of his dreams"* (Genesis 37:19, 20).

This innocent young man walked majestically towards his brothers; brothers in whom he had all confidence would protect him should any eventuality occur. His mind was clear of any evil intent from his brothers; all he did was just putting the message from his father into shape. While, with clear conscience he walked towards his own siblings, evil was lurking on the other side of the line. Joseph wouldn't have believed if someone had told him such a heinous crime had been cooked and was about to be perpetrated against him by his own flesh and blood. But it was real, they had planned to do it, and yes, they did it in a way that concealed any evidence of foul play.

> *So when Joseph came to his brothers, they stripped him of his robe - the ornate robe he was wearing - and they took him and threw him into the cistern. The cistern was empty; there was no water in it (Genesis 37:23 24).*

After stripping him of his coat of many colors, the brothers, at this material moment, did not know exactly what to do with Joseph. They were attempting to prevent the dream - his reign over them - from coming to pass. They debated among themselves what should be done to him. They traded ideas back and forth. Finally, they all, with the exception of Reuben, came to a consensus that he should be killed. Reuben was against the whole idea and was planning for an alternative. Reuben wanted to save him and send him back to the father, this resulted in another round of hot argument. It forced Reuben to excuse himself from them.

> *As they sat down to eat their meal, they looked up and saw a caravan of Ishmaelites coming from Gilead. Their camels were loaded with spices, balm and myrrh, and they were on their way to take them down to Egypt (Genesis 37:25).*

Out of nowhere, Judah changed his mind when he saw the caravan of the merchants coming. Surprisingly,

> *Judah said to his brothers, "What will we gain if we kill our brother and cover up his blood? Come, let's sell him to the Ishmaelites and not lay our hands on him; after all, he is our brother, our own flesh and blood." His brothers agreed (Genesis 37: 26, 27).*

When it came to what amount they should receive for Joseph, each one chipped in a suggestion or two. This interaction went on among them for some time. Since it was a sinister and a heinous idea, they were in haste to dispose of the 'merchandise' they did not pay anything for.

> *So when the Midianite merchants came by, his brothers pulled Joseph up out of the cistern and sold him for twenty shekels of silver to the Ishmaelites, who took him to Egypt (Genesis 37:28).*

In Reuben's absence, they sold their brother. They sold him not for any huge amount of money that would be commensurate with human life, but for a pittance: twenty shekels of silver. This was almost the same as the amount Judas Iscariot gambled for the life of Jesus.

> *Then one of the Twelve - the one called Judas Iscariot - went to the chief priests and asked, "What are you willing to give me if I deliver him over to you?" So they counted out for him thirty pieces of silver (Matthew 26:14, 15).*

Every effort Joseph made to convince his brothers not to sell him into slavery proved futile. His submissions were to no avail. His fate and future were in the hands of these buyers. What was going to happen to him he could not fathom.

> *When Reuben returned to the cistern and saw that Joseph was not there, he tore his clothes. He went back to his brothers and said, "The boy isn't there! Where can I turn now?" Then they got Joseph's robe, slaughtered a goat and dipped the robe in the blood. They took the ornate robe back to their father and said, "We found this. Examine it to see whether it is your son's robe (Genesis 37:29-32).*

And therefore, Joseph's coat - made of many colors - made for him by his loving father was stripped off from his back. He was deprived of a treasure. Yes, a treasured part of him had been torn away. But though Joseph's coat might be stripped off, the dreamer and the giver of the dream were still alive. This episode was the beginning of the stripping of his first coat and the subsequent ones he would wear.

FOOD FOR THOUGHT

- ➢ What would have happened if Jacob had not sent Joseph after his brothers?
- ➢ What if Joseph had refused to go on that errand for the father?

- What if Joseph had returned home when he didn't see them in Shechem?
- What if Joseph had resisted the brothers and therefore could not be sold?
- What if he freed himself from the Ishmaelite merchants and ran to the father?

Chapter Two

THE SECOND COAT

"Do not plot harm against your neighbor, who lives trustfully near you. Do not accuse anyone for no reason — when they have done you no harm" (Proverbs 3:29, 30).

When the head, the heart and the hand have nothing to do, the evil one finds something for them to be engaged in. So, one must make every effort to always put them to work. David failed to realize this kind of wisdom and fell victim to the devil's sinister plot. This was David's plight that evening when he walked the rooftop of his palace. It caused him to go where he was not supposed to, do what he was not supposed to do and then devise an evil plan to execute a loyal citizen who was so dedicated to the course of God and to David himself. The death of Uriah left blood stains in David's hand. An incident resulting in devastating consequences that were too difficult to gather, the gathered pieces too numerous to count.

It was the period when kings go to war to defend and protect their territories. David was no exception to this trend. But he shelved his responsibility, instead sending Joab, his commander, to take his place. One evening, as David walked around his palace rooftop, he saw a beautiful woman bathing and sent for her. David had an affair with her which resulted in the woman taking seed. The woman was Bathsheba and she was Uriah's wife. The king had taken someone's wife and gotten her pregnant. Rumors surrounding this horrible event began to swell. To allow the brunt of shame from his action fall on him would be too difficult to bear. David set in motion a distinct but wicked plan to get Uriah implicated in the pregnancy and tag him with it. He invited Uriah from the battlefield, his intention being to persuade him to sleep with his wife. In the end, he would be responsible for the pregnancy and David would be exonerated. He would be free from any obligation. Uriah responded to the king when he got the message but David's plan could not materialize. Every effort and every push proved futile. Uriah responded to the king's machinations and is recorded thus:

> *Uriah said to David, "The ark and Israel and Judah are staying in tents, and my commander Joab and my lord's men are camped in the open country. How could I go to my house to eat and drink and make love to my wife? As surely as you live, I will not do such a thing!" (2 Samuel 11:11).*

With this solemn response, David realized he was losing the charge over the game by the minute and he decided to shift it in a different direction. As failure stared intensely at him, David threatened Uriah with sending him back to the war front. He did, and did it wickedly. He put into Uriah's own hands his 'death warrant.' The content called on Joab to execute a plan by putting him in the fiercest part of the war. Joab obeyed the king and Uriah met his untimely death.

Joseph, perceiving the destructive effect from such an act, did not bow to that cruel demand of his master's wife. So she falsely accused him. And it ended him in a cold dungeon. What David couldn't resist, Joseph did. Though they all faced consequences for their various decisions, Joseph's resulted in exaltation to a high position. How did it all happen?

(A) The Giving of the Second Coat (Gen. 39:3-6)

The sky's view from where Joseph was sitting on the donkey was captivating. This scene gave a picturesque beauty of God's creation. The sun was solemnly setting across the horizon. Its rays had dispersed through the clouds but reluctantly, as if scared or shy of its existence. Though this dispersion of the sun's rays seemed to be imperfect, it still encouraged the merchants to pursue their journey with the utmost dignity they thought it deserved.

They talked of the hectic schedules they had endured since they started this business expedition. What they hoped to achieve, and thereafter invest the profit into other business ventures, occupied their time. Among them was infuriated Joseph who was against the whole encounter. He sat quietly, thinking of the betrayal he had just experienced in the hands of his own blood brothers. He resented the brothers' idea of selling him off to a far foreign land and a people he had no previous knowledge of. A people whose culture differs from what he had known all his life: the food, dressings, religion and other host of doing things. A thought came into his mind and he decided to talk over his predicament with the merchants, maybe they might be convinced to let him go. He attempted so many times to get them to reason up with him to accept the reason why they shouldn't have bought him. He told them of his family, the death of his mother while giving birth to his younger brother, his father's old age and what his absence would cost him. He tried any and every reason he found convincing but never succeeded. His demeanor was louder than words could articulate. Failure staring at him squarely he felt helpless and hopeless, resentful and agitated when he realized his freedom was beyond any human intervention. With a heavy heart, he bowed his head down and away from their sight, he said a silent prayer, saying:

Lord, how many are my foes! How many rise up against me! Many are saying of me, "God will not deliver him." But you, Lord, are a shield around me, my glory, the One who lifts my head high. I call out to the Lord, and he answers me from his holy mountain. I lie down and sleep; I wake again because the Lord sustains me. I will not fear though tens of thousands assail me on every side. Arise, Lord! Deliver me, my God! Strike all my enemies on the jaw; break the teeth of the wicked. From the Lord comes deliverance. May your blessing be on your people (Psalm 3:1-8).

Now it was dawn, and the crows of the cocks from the hamlets dotted along the path, announcing the arrival of a new day. A day they all anticipated to be favorable as far as their business transactions were concerned. They walked briskly, and with usual purpose towards the town square. They had just crossed the river and the entourage was now at the edge of the town. They saw town folks going to and coming from the river; the only source of the village's water supply. Their feet collecting dust from the journey, hence, the plan to stop along the way to wash these feet. Joseph did not include himself in their plans, and he could not be. He listened to every word as they contemplated over many issues. But their point of call - where they would dispose of their goods - was the main one that took the most time for their discussions.

As was their custom, they put their heads together as to how they would dispose of the slave in their possession.

While some suggested they keep him for some time, others wanted him sold immediately. It was in the middle of this ongoing discussion that it really dawned on Joseph of the plight that had befallen him. Out of desperation, he demanded from God to "Answer me when I call to you, my righteous God. Give me relief from my distress; have mercy on me and hear my prayer" (Psalm 4:1). His fears had become a reality. "Where is God in this whole drama?" He began to query himself. "Was the dream really true? Or was it just an illusion?" Doubt began to creep into his life slowly. He couldn't have fathomed the events playing before his eyes as real if he had been told. Then there was patter of feet behind him. Out of curiosity, he turned to look at what was going on. What his eyes set on was so shocking. They were coming to take him to the slave market to be sold. His heart leaped and, pain without any measure, cut through his tiny chest. He did not hesitate to go with them because had no choice. Joseph accepted his plight and decided to get the best out of it. It was a painful experience, it was traumatizing. Joseph did not put up any resistance at all, he followed them to the block for the early morning slave inspection from prospective buyers. A few buyers stopped to appraise him but were discouraged by his tiny and bony structure. For three consecutive days, this scenario played before him. It looked like no one wanted him in their house.

But the third day was to change his plight. Getting to the close of the day, Potiphar made his way to the slave market. He walked sternly, inspecting every slave along his path. He saw tall and short, fat and skinny, strong and weak yet none appealed to him. After an exhaustive search, he was planning to give up but for the timely intervention of an acquaintance. This friend suggested he should go a little further. Potiphar brushed him off at first. But this friend insisted, prodded and pointed him in Joseph's direction. He finally listened and left. When he had reached where Joseph was, he examined him thoroughly. And having been satisfied, he bargained for him. It did not take any time long when the owners closed the deal with Potiphar. In the time of the bargaining, Joseph heard some of the slave sellers tout Potiphar's credentials. So, with all the respect due him as an officer in the king's army, Joseph followed him to his house. From pain and anguish, Joseph spoke these words in prayer:

> *Have mercy on me, Lord, for I am faint; heal me, Lord, for my bones are in agony. My soul is in deep anguish. How long, Lord, how long? Turn, Lord, and deliver me; save me because of your unfailing love. Among the dead no one proclaims your name. Who praises you from the grave? I am worn out from my groaning. All night long I flood my bed with weeping and drench my couch with tears (Psalm 6:2-6).*

Potiphar took him home and Joseph served him. He served with distinction. He served without any malice or prejudice. Joseph was just responding to the call that

> *Slaves, obey your earthly masters in everything; and do it, not only when their eye is on you and to curry their favor, but with sincerity of heart and reverence for the Lord. Whatever you do, work at it with all your heart, as working for the Lord, not for human masters, since you know that you will receive an inheritance from the Lord as a reward. It is the Lord Christ you are serving (Colossians 3:22-24).*

It was not long time after, when Potiphar noticed the change in his household ever since Joseph stepped his two feet on his compound. Having discussed with his wife, Potiphar took a bold decision and he made Joseph the head of his household, ahead of some of the folks who were serving there before Joseph was brought in.

Joseph found favor in his eyes and became his attendant. Potiphar put him in charge of his household, and he entrusted to his care everything he owned. From the time he put him in charge of his household and of all that he owned, the Lord blessed the household of the Egyptian because of Joseph. The blessing of the Lord was on everything Potiphar had, both in the house and in the field. So, Potiphar left everything he had in Joseph's care; with Joseph in charge, he did not concern himself with anything except the food he ate… (Genesis 39:4-6).

Here we can infer Joseph received his second coat, for being the head of the household and of the other slaves. A coat that would distinguish him from the other servants in the entire household.

(B) The Stripping of the Second Coat (Gen.39:13, 14)

How did it all happen one would ask? As we realized at this juncture, Joseph was bought to serve in Potiphar's house. He sent him to his army quarters. Joseph was to serve him, but even there the Lord was with him. The Lord blessed him so that whatever he touched prospered (Genesis 39:2). He developed in strength and with wisdom. Potiphar noticed the difference ever since Joseph became part of his household. Having realized that, Potiphar left everything under his care except his wife.

With this new-found success at whatever Joseph's hands touched, came along with the plot by the devil to derail everything he gained. Success can affect one's output, most especially in ministry. And if we are not careful we could be swayed away easily from the call of God. It is for this reason Peter cautioned believers thus to be aware of the schemes of the enemy;

> *Be alert and of sober mind. Your enemy the devil prowls around like a roaring lion looking for someone to devour. Resist him, standing firm in the faith, because you know that the family of believers throughout the world is undergoing the same kind of sufferings (1Peter 5:8, 9).*

Joseph knew the devil's schemes, so he continued to build good relationship with his God. But the devil was not perturbed by that strong relationship he continued to develop with God. The devil pursued him constantly in order that Joseph might fall prey to his machinations. Potiphar's wife was the instrument he decided to use. With his position as the head caretaker of the household, he frequented the main quarters where his master and the wife resided. The wife took notice of Joseph's masculine-built body. There, this feeling of seduction began to invade her mind and body. With her position in the society as a commander's wife, she should have considered the implications, but she did not. She made advances towards him. Her feelings for the young man were so strong that she couldn't any way restrain herself. Her appetite, and her desire to satisfy this strong feeling clouded her judgment. Her request, Joseph must to come to bed with her.

> *Can a man scoop fire into his lap without his clothes being burned? Can a man walk on hot coals without his feet being scorched? So is he who sleeps with another man's wife; no one who touches her will go unpunished (Proverbs 6:27-29).*

Joseph was aware of the devastating consequences should he succumb to her plot. So, Joseph refused every request and resisted every advance she made to seduce him. But with every refusal and resistance came with a corresponding persistence from his master's wife. And he also met her resistance with a counter resistance. The situation became complicated for the Jewish young man and seemed to be getting out of hand. He found himself stuck in a sticky situation without knowing what exactly he was supposed to do. The young man's confusion gave her the courage to continue with her wicked plot. Having gone on for some time and tired of giving excuses, Joseph mustered courage to confront her head on. He boldly told her,

> *"With me in charge," he told her, "my master does not concern himself with anything in the house; everything he owns he has entrusted to my care. No one is greater in this house than I am. My master has withheld nothing from me except you, because you are his wife. How then could I do such a wicked thing and sin against God?" (Genesis 39:8, 9).*

In whatever manner, she might have understood Joseph's reluctance to condone, but on this fateful day, she purposed to execute her plan. His world was about to turn upside down. The normal and peaceful life he lived was about to be disrupted. He went, as usual, to the main quarters to perform his daily chores. He never thought anything sinister was in the making or would happen to him. Like the previous occasions, she invited him to come to bed with her this morning again. He refused to compromise. He brushed her flirtatious gestures aside as if he did not notice her antics. To his surprise, his master's wife grabbed his coat and pulled him towards her with all strength she could gather. She held on to the lapel end of his coat, combining cohesion and persuasion to urge him to give in. Joseph resisted, while he also struggled to free himself from her grip he never succeeded. With strength coming from nowhere, this God-fearing young man ran away leaving his coat in the hands of his master's wife. Panting profusely after freeing himself from her grip, he exited the room without looking back. "I have overcome her once again," he said to himself silently. Though he freed himself, it would cost him something. It cost him of his coat being stripped from his back that fateful day. He hurriedly headed straight to his side of the quarters. He went and sat down quietly, trying to make head and tail of what had just happened to him. Reflecting upon events as he sat alone by himself, he knew he was in a big trouble.

It was evening when the door opened with its usual accompanying hinges noise. There, Potiphar entered with his retinue of body guards trailing him. They saluted him when he fully entered his abode. The guards turned away, leaving him in the middle of his sitting room. Huddled in the corner of the sitting room and covered with her blue quilt, Potiphar's wife shook as if death was beckoning her. Her upper and lower sets of teeth were hitting each other in attempt to justify her allegations she was about to level against Joseph. The absence of the usual hug from his wife sent a signal to him. He dashed with love and great admiration to the seat beside her. Potiphar hardly sat down when his wife approached him with the lies she concocted out of shame. She reported Joseph to her husband. She overwhelmingly skipped the whole truth of the matter.

> *Then she told him this story: "That Hebrew slave you brought us came to me to make sport of me. But as soon as I screamed for help, he left his cloak beside me and ran out of the house. When his master heard the story his wife told him, saying, "This is how your slave treated me," he burned with anger. Joseph's master took him and put him in prison, the place where the king's prisoners were confined... (Genesis 39:17-20).*

Potiphar was disappointed when the story was narrated and became frustrated. What decision was he supposed to take? That was the big question that lingered on his mind since the whole incident revolved around Joseph. He trusted him and knew the Lord was with him. The coat was there in her hand to prove his guilt, but beneath, he doubted a little bit. Though there were holes in her story yet, there was a mountain of evidence to prove his guilt. "It is disgusting for such a thing to happen under my roof," he soliloquized. He was confused but he nor anyone attempted to investigate so the whole truth of the story could be unearthed. For that matter, nobody came forward to corroborate Joseph's version of the incident.

Joseph stood there alone trying to prove his innocence. He attempted to call a fellow servant in the household, in whom he confided with some of his wife's frequent demand for this illicit affair. The accusation leveled against Joseph captured the attention of the whole household. The household was gripped with fear and shock, and was subdued by shame and perplexity. No one dared offer any alternative view regarding Joseph's integrity and innocence. They saw his hands being tied with a rope behind him. They saw Joseph being whisked away for a crime he did not commit but was falsely accused of. He was not given the opportunity to defend himself. They saw the two guards on both sides guarding him as they walked to the prison. Joseph was dumped in the prison without any proper trial.

Within a few hours, his status changed dramatically. His place of abode in Potiphar's house being traded for a prison cell. He was stripped of, not only of his position as the one in charge, but the coat that identified him as the head. Sitting on the edge of the prison bed this first night, this thought came into his mind. He identified with Job:

If only my anguish could be weighed and all my misery be placed on the scales! It would surely outweigh the sand of the seas - no wonder my words have been impetuous (Job 6:2, 3).

The dungeon would be his home for God-knows-when period, and there was nothing he could do to effect a change to his situation. Joseph would have to accept his predicament and, yes, he did. But truth be told, it was not as easy as we might have imagined. Yet, as he sat there brooding over the whole episode, he hummed this song in his mind so he could find some solace;

Through It All

I've had many tears and sorrows,
I've had questions for tomorrow,
there's been times I didn't know right from wrong.
But in every situation,
God gave me blessed consolation,
that my trials come to only make me strong.

Through it all,
through it all,
I've learned to trust in Jesus,
I've learned to trust in God.

Through it all,
through it all,
I've learned to depend upon His Word.

I've been to lots of places,
I've seen a lot of faces,
there's been times I felt so all alone.
But in my lonely hours,
yes, those precious lonely hours,
Jesus lets me know that I was His own

Through it all,
through it all,
I've learned to trust in Jesus,
I've learned to trust in God.

Through it all,
through it all,
I've learned to depend upon His Word.

I thank God for the mountains,
and I thank Him for the valleys,
I thank Him for the storms He brought me through.
For if I'd never had a problem,
I wouldn't know God could solve them,
I'd never know what faith in God could do.
--Andrae Crouch

FOOD FOR THOUGHT

> ➤ Why didn't Joseph just compromise with her for the demands she made?

- What would have happened if he compromised?
- Wouldn't the compromise work to his benefit?

The Second Coat

Chapter Three

THE THIRD COAT

"This is what the LORD says: 'Curse is the one who trusts in man, who depends on flesh for his strength and whose heart turns away from the LORD'" (Jeremiah 17:5).

The days of His crucifixion was drawing nearer by the day. Every hour, every minute and every second, that historical event drew nearer than before. And Jesus was aware of the atrocities that were going to be visited upon Him through the hands of the Jewish leaders. So, He began to speak directly about this episode to the apostles and the disciples following him. He followed that with prayers for them and the believers that would come thereafter. When He had finished praying, He motioned His followers to head towards the Kidron Valley. Beside this deep valley was a beautiful garden. They settled there for further communion among themselves. Judas knew Jesus and the apostles had often met there. The Bible records that

> *Judas came to the garden, guiding a detachment of soldiers and some officials from the chief priests and the Pharisees. They were carrying torches, lanterns and weapons. Jesus, knowing all that was going to happen to him, went out and asked them, "Who is it you want?" "Jesus of Nazareth," they replied (John 18:3-5).*

Thus, Jesus was arrested, betrayed by a bosom friend. The friend with whom He walked the same dusted road, with whom He ate from the same bowl and with whom He slept on open fields. The person, who was supposed to defend Him, instead gave Him up, for fees that did not commensurate His worth. Judas so soon forgot Jesus' good deed when He rescued their lives in that fiery raging storm. So was Joseph's experience in the dungeon, forgotten by one whose encounter with him should never have been forgotten.

(A) The Giving of the Third Coat (Gen. 39:22-23)

As Joseph sat in the corner of the dungeon, reminiscing about the events of the past few years, the December mid-winter wind blew outside sturdily and forced its way into the dungeon through the holes above serving as ventilation. This, therefore, speeded the dungeon temperature to fall below normal this time in the past years. Many questions flooded his mind at this juncture. Questions that had baffled him ever since he was sold: "Where is the God our ancestors talked about? Where are the attributes we were told of each day?" These questions begged for answers that were not readily available. Gideon posited similar questions when he interacted with God on this same issue.

> *"Pardon me, my lord," Gideon replied, "but if the Lord is with us, why has all this happened to us? Where are all his wonders that our ancestors told us about when they said, 'Did not the Lord bring us up out of Egypt?' But now the Lord has abandoned us and given us into the hand of Midian (Judges 6:13).*

Joseph was caught up in a similar trap of doubt. He was traumatized, confused, agitated and discouraged by happenings since he left home that fateful morning long ago to run his father's errand. Joseph could still hear his father's voice as he cautioned him to be careful and vigilant during the journey he was undertaking. He remembered vividly the very words his father spoke, and that of his when he responded in affirmation. He could still recognize the love which his father, Jacob, jealously guarded for him in his words. He could not wrap his mind around the whole controversy. It looked like he was day-dreaming, but it was real. This was a real life event happening to a real person. Then he remembered his father once said, "Do not plot harm against your neighbor, who lives trustfully near you. Do not accuse anyone for no reason - when they have done you no harm" (Proverbs

3:29, 30). Could this proverb sooth his pain a little bit? No, it did not. Even with the prevailing cold, Joseph had beads of sweat gathered on his forehead. His heart pounded his chest as if it wanted to rip it apart. "Why? What have I done to deserve this kind of treatment?" he asked rhetorically. Joseph's hope seemed to be fading, his faith seemed to be ebbing and his confidence seemed to be waning by the day. "Life is cruel," he was saying it to himself but there was this still voice whispering into his ears saying,

> *Before I formed you in the womb I knew you, before you were born I set you apart; I appointed you as a prophet to the nations [therefore, be assured] ... I know the plans I have for you," declares the Lord, 'plans to prosper you and not to harm you, plans to give you hope and a future' (Jeremiah 1:5; 29:11).*

Joseph's predicament grew from bad to worse. He never anticipated being accused of a crime he did not commit, and never to be allowed to defend himself but thrown into a cold dungeon. His patience with God was running out, doubt was setting in, and invariably affected his view of God. And though that day changed his view, He, the almighty God, did not change His view about Joseph. God's view was described this way;

> *But while Joseph was there in the prison, the Lord was with him; he showed him kindness and granted him favor in the*

eyes of the prison warden. So the warden put Joseph in charge of all those held in the prison, and he was made responsible for all that was done there (Genesis 39:20 -22).

It had been just a few months after Joseph was admitted into the prison system when the chief warden realized he possessed exceptional qualities. The warden assigned him to take responsibility for the daily running of the prison, and Joseph performed that assignment from then onwards. Joseph was again placed in a leadership position. He was given another coat to differentiate him from the other prisoners and his new coat gave him a new identity. He was the head prisoner. A position he occupied with honor and grace, dignity and humility. The Lord was with him as he took care of events in the prison. As a result, "The warden paid no attention to anything under Joseph's care, because the Lord was with Joseph and gave him success in whatever he did" (Genesis 39:23). Even in the prison, the presence of God was with him all along.

(B) The Stripping of the Third Coat (Gen. 41:14)

This morning was not different from what they had known and experienced over the months. It was not usual for the warden to go around and check on the prison inmates. But the summons that morning from the warden for his presence as the prison guards stood behind the prison gate seemed odd. It was not the time for the prisoners to go out and stretch, yet he was being called by the warden. Since there was no excuse for him not to respond, he followed the guard sent to him. As they bent the second corner, he saw two well-dressed gentlemen sitting at the other side of the prison. The warden introduced them to Joseph as the cupbearer and the baker of the king. He therefore charged Joseph to serve them. From then, and onward through the few months that they spent in the prison, he attended to their needs. It was said that,

> Sometime later, the cupbearer and the baker of the king of Egypt offended their master, the king of Egypt. Pharaoh was angry with his two officials, the chief cupbearer and the chief baker, and put them in custody in the house of the captain of the guard, in the same prison where Joseph was confined. The captain of the guard assigned them to Joseph, and he attended them... (Genesis 40:1-4).

One afternoon, they sat and chatted over the issues that brought them into the prison while Joseph sat there and listened with all the attention he could gather. They reminiscence over the memorable experiences they enjoyed in the palace. Like the Pharaoh's meeting with kings from other kingdoms. Joseph did not contribute any input. He stayed put out of his reverence for their high positions.

The following morning when Joseph went to attend to them, he realized that the palace officials' demeanor had changed. A sorrowful demeanor, unfortunately they never recognized themselves. Joseph, being a concerned human being, enquired from them of that sad mood.

> *When Joseph came to them the next morning, he saw that they were dejected. So he asked Pharaoh's officials who were in custody with him in his master's house, "Why do you look so sad today?" "We both had dreams," they answered, "but there is no one to interpret them." Then Joseph said to them, "Do not interpretations belong to God? Tell me your dreams (Genesis 40:6-8).*

When he heard their dreams, Joseph became silent. His silence conveyed a different message. They mistook his silence to mean his inability. Then to their surprise, Joseph accepted to help. Immediately there was a relief when Joseph opted to interpret their dreams. A burden had rolled off their shoulders. The cupbearer, who chose to go first told of his dream, giving all the details Joseph needed to know. Without any hesitation, Joseph assured him he knew the meaning of the dream and went on to explain to him what it meant. After Joseph had finished with the cupbearer's interpretation, he followed it with a request of his own. He said,

> *But when all goes well with you, remember me and show me kindness; mention me to Pharaoh and get me out of this prison. I was forcibly carried off from the land of the Hebrews, and even here I have done nothing to deserve being put in a dungeon (Genesis 40:14, 15).*

The content was very encouraging to the baker. Without wasting any time, he also narrated his dream to Joseph. Joseph was again on hand to interpret his too. He did, and no one should deserve such a dream. Three days from the day, the dreams manifested as Joseph said. The cupbearer was restored to his position in the palace and the baker was killed just as he gave the interpretations.

> *Now the third day was Pharaoh's birthday, and he gave a feast for all his officials. He lifted up the heads of the chief cupbearer and the chief baker in the presence of his officials: He restored the chief cupbearer to his position, so that he once again put the cup into Pharaoh's hand— but he impaled the chief baker, just as Joseph had said to them in his interpretation (Genesis 40:20-22).*

The Pharaoh's birthday celebration demanded the presence of his officials. In lieu of that, the chief cupbearer was required to be present. Pharaoh ordered his immediate release. So, a retinue of palace guards was dispatched to bring him from the prison back to the palace. The news shocked him but he was elated. The cupbearer was aware of the important role Joseph played in his life. So, when he was leaving the prison, he gave Joseph a solemn promise he would raise his issue up with the Pharaoh. He swore to move heaven and earth not to forget him. Instead, the opposite happened. The Bible says, "The chief cupbearer, however, did not remember Joseph; he forgot him" (Genesis 40:23). Joseph was left alone in the prison to fend for his life and plight. There was no hope as the days went by. He received no word from the palace. And there were reasons for him to doubt if ever he would be released.

Two years have passed since the chief cupbearer left the prison. Then God intervened so the Pharaoh could have a dream which no one could interpret. The cupbearer then remembered his promise made to Joseph some two years ago. He recommended Joseph to the Pharaoh. The Pharaoh ordered Joseph release and summoned him into his presence. He was thus stripped of his third coat; coat of authority and position in the prison. What happened next after this stripping?

FOOD FOR THOUGHT

- ➢ What would have happened if Potiphar had not bought Joseph?
- ➢ Would Joseph have been tempted by another woman?
- ➢ Would that accusation had sent him to king's prison?
- ➢ Would he have met the baker and the butler?
- ➢ Would he have been introduced to Pharaoh?

Chapter Four

THE LAST COAT

"And we know that in all things God works for the good of those who love him, who have been called according to his purpose" (Romans 8:28).

The church by this time, was thriving beyond imagination. The Lord was adding new members to their number by the day. Members who previously were worshipping idols and therefore making money for their masters, left and followed Jesus. Their conversions caused a stir in their enterprises, with their bosses and in the professional circles. The courage displayed by the Apostles emboldened the disciples to share the good news to whoever would listen. The popularity of the leadership and the mass flocking towards them seemed to affect King Herod. His base was shaken by the boldness being displayed by folks considered illiterates. Then the king issued threats against this new wind of message blowing across the land but it could not be deterred.

> *Remember what I told you: 'A servant is not greater than his master.' If they persecuted me, they will persecute you also. If they obeyed my teaching, they will obey yours also. They will treat you this way because of my name, for they do not know the one who sent me (John 15:20-21).*

The Apostles were clearly aware of Jesus' cautions whiles He was with them. They were ready for any eventualities. The various masters of the servants did not take it kindly at all with the Apostles' success. So, King Herod joined forces with these masters to take a stand against this new movement.

King Herod's modus operandi was to infiltrate their ranks, cause confusion and then eliminate them one after the other. He took it upon himself to lead in the destruction of this movement. His main objective was to have this movement wiped out, and he wouldn't have to compete with the new King the Apostles were propagating. Therefore, he had James, the brother of John the beloved, arrested and killed. The rippling effect went as far as the ears of the Jewish authorities. Herod caught the wind that they were happy about the execution of James. With this encouragement, he went on to arrest Peter. He would make him the next victim of his wicked intentions. Luke narrated the incident thus;

> *When he saw that this met with approval among the Jews, he proceeded to seize Peter also. This happened during the*

Festival of Unleavened Bread. After arresting him, he put him in prison, handing him over to be guarded by four squads of four soldiers each. Herod intended to bring him out for public trial after the Passover (Acts 12:3, 4).

Herod designed all plans to be put into effect after the Passover. The plan to do away with Peter. He had every detail set out for the execution of this man of God. "There was no way I would not succeed in executing this scheme," he might have assured himself. He assured himself of eliminating them one after the other so 'The Way' could be wiped out. But the king was not aware that "Many are the plans in a person's heart, but it is the Lord's purpose that prevails" (Proverbs 19:21). Herod had no inclination the Lord was ahead of him. That the Lord would use his very decision to achieve His purpose. Then the Lord set His rescue plan in motion to thwart the schemes of this evil man. He sent an angel on this mission to release Peter. It is said,

> *Suddenly an angel of the Lord appeared and a light shone in the cell. He struck Peter on the side and woke him up. "Quick, get up!" he said, and the chains fell off Peter's wrists. Then the angel said to him, "Put on your clothes and sandals." And Peter did so. "Wrap your cloak around you and follow me," the angel told him. Peter followed him out of the prison, but he had no idea that what the angel was doing was really happening; he thought he was seeing a vision. They passed the first and second guards and came to the iron gate leading to the city. It opened for them by itself,*

> *and they went through it. When they had walked the length of one street, suddenly the angel left him. Then Peter came to himself and said, "Now I know without a doubt that the Lord has sent his angel and rescued me from Herod's clutches and from everything the Jewish people were hoping would happen" (Acts 12:7-11).*

When the King had finally sat on his throne that morning, he was elated about his orchestrations. He was very determined to put fears into this movement and stop them. So, without wasting any more time, he ordered Peter be brought to stand trial. Obeying the king's command, the soldiers rushed to the prison but to their surprise, Peter was nowhere to be found. Every effort to retrace his whereabout yielded no result. The prison guards combed everywhere in the prison but came up empty-handed. The tide immediately changed. They had become the victims, instead of the victors. The news was related to the king. Peter's absence from the prison caused a great uproar in the palace. The King flew into rage and spewed his anger in every direction. King Herod tempers flared and shot high. As a result, he demanded immediate arrest of all the guards and they were duly executed. The confusion in Herod's camp was reminiscent of what happened in the court of the Pharaoh's palace when he had the dream and his spiritual men could not come out with anything meaningful.

All attempts to understand the dreams, as the Pharaoh sat on the edge of his bed, eluded him. *"What are the meanings of these dreams?"* he kept asking himself while he drifted into another round of sleep. Though he found it very tough to sleep, at the end, he did. Comparing this night to the ones before, this was not a pleasant one for him. He woke up early this morning. He was gripped with fear from the dreams.

In the palace this morning, the Pharaoh was adorned with ornaments made from the purest gold. He sat on the throne that fateful morning with pageantry. All the servants in the palace were at their posts, performing their duties with the utmost precisions they deserved. The very first thing he did was to assemble his wise men, enchanters and magicians so they could give him the meaning of the dreams. He narrated the dream to the assembly of his wise men. The Bible recounts it this way:

> *When two full years had passed, Pharaoh had a dream: He was standing by the Nile, when out of the river there came up seven cows, sleek and fat, and they grazed among the reeds. After them, seven other cows, ugly and gaunt, came up out of the Nile and stood beside those on the riverbank. And the cows that were ugly and gaunt ate up the seven sleek, fat cows. Then Pharaoh woke up. He fell asleep again and had a second dream: Seven heads of grain, healthy and good, were growing on a single stalk. After them, seven other heads of grain sprouted - thin and scorched by the east wind.*

> *The thin heads of grain swallowed up the seven healthy, full heads. Then Pharaoh woke up; it had been a dream. In the morning his mind was troubled, so he sent for all the magicians and wise men of Egypt. Pharaoh told them his dreams, but no one could interpret them for him (Genesis 41:1-8).*

Their inability to do his bidding threw him into a tirade. He fumed with rage and resentment. The kingmakers sat there quietly with their eyes sternly fixed on him. A loud silence pervaded the whole palace while he ranted and vented his anger at the enchanters and magicians. No one dared to interrupt, and no one did. Pharaoh was confused, perplexed and irritated since no tangible answer seemed to be coming forth. He was left all alone to do the ranting but when he had calmed down after the rounds of this bitter denunciation, he asked of what should be the next move. The silence continued. Everyone seemed to be scared. No one would want to irk him any further. There was a servant directly behind him with a big fan in his hands. He was fanning the king with all the strength he could muster, yet it made no difference with how he was feeling. Pockets of sweat began to gather on his forehead and in his palm. The cupbearer, whom Joseph had not seen for the past two years, was standing on the Pharaoh's left side. He was holding a golden cup ready to deliver should he be asked. The palace elders sat in a row on his right hand. They consulted each other regarding the pending issue; the interpretation of the dreams. It was in the middle of this turmoil that the chief cupbearer remembered the dream he had in the prison; its interpretation and fulfilment. Without any hesitation, he immediately related it to the Pharaoh saying;

> *"Today I am reminded of my shortcomings. Pharaoh was once angry with his servants, and he imprisoned me and the chief baker in the house of the captain of the guard. Each of us had a dream the same night, and each dream had a meaning of its own. Now a young Hebrew was there with us, a servant of the captain of the guard. We told him our dreams, and he interpreted them for us, giving each man the interpretation of his dream. And things turned out exactly as he interpreted them to us: I was restored to my position, and the other man was impaled" (Genesis 41:9-13).*

Pharaoh and his elders were skeptical about the chief cupbearer's assertion at the beginning. They did not believe him, for no one ever mentioned it in the palace. *"How could a human being interpret a dream the gods of our land could not?"* This was the question that made rounds yet, they could not find answers to. They, including the Pharaoh, doubted the testimony. They wanted to brush it away so they could find solution elsewhere. But one kinsman suggested, since the wise men, the magicians and the enchanters could not do what was required of them, they should just give the cupbearer's suggestion a try since time was racing against them. The Pharaoh's patience was running out. They deliberated over the suggestion for just a few minutes then they came to a consensus to give it a try. So there and then, the Pharaoh ordered Joseph to be brought.

That morning, Joseph played back the event that happened a few years ago, culminating in his imprisonment. And he said it silently to himself, *"I was accused of attempting to rape my master's wife. I am going to die in this dungeon and none of my family members will ever be aware of the whole story behind it."* These thoughts flashed through his mind while sitting on the bare ground that fateful morning. He thought of it over and over many times yet, he couldn't make any good sense out of it all. It had been two full years but he received no word from the cupbearer as he vehemently pledged and promised to. Every day, Joseph looked forward to hearing news from the palace for his release, or at least, for his case to be heard. Nothing was received in return for the services he rendered the chief cupbearer. Joseph's plight was in limbo and that caused him to think of his future, which in his eyes, looked bleak. The solution to his situation seemed not to be in sight, and if there was any at all, it was very far away from materializing any time soon. Discouragement had set in and resulted in total confusion. At this moment, his organized life seemed to be spiraling into a confused chasm of helplessness and hopelessness. God was silent and, it had been so for some time now. But He was working behind the scenes. He was scheming His ways to establish a fact; that He is the one calling the shots. There and then Joseph prayed this prayer;

> *The Lord is my shepherd, I lack nothing. He makes me lie down in green pastures, he leads me beside quiet waters, he refreshes my soul. He guides me along the right paths for his name's sake. Even though I walk through the darkest valley I will fear no evil, for you are with me; your rod and your staff, they comfort me (Psalm 23: 1-4).*

His flesh seemed to be winning the war against the Spirit. He needed a jolt from somewhere. Without the slightest hesitation, the Lord responded with the words He sent to Paul in his trying moment; the same words of encouragement. The Bible recorded thus:

> *One night the Lord spoke to Paul in a vision: "Do not be afraid; keep on speaking, do not be silent. For I am with you, and no one is going to attack and harm you, because I have many people in this city" (Acts 18:9, 19).*

There was nothing so particular about that day; nothing so special that it shouldn't be taken for granted. But it was not normal for the palace guards to come to the prison. In fact, it was a breach of royal protocol. So, when Joseph saw the two guards standing at his prison gate, his heart leapt as if it were coming out of his chest. He got scared of their presence, most especially when he became aware of the reason. The palace guard informed Joseph the demand for his presence in the palace with these words; "Pharaoh wants you in the palace right away." His experience with his brothers and Potiphar's wife suddenly rushed to the fore. Shocked and shaking, Joseph immediately shot back with these questions; *"What again have I done? Why am I wanted in the palace? Has someone made any allegation against me again?"* He flooded the guards with series of questions without bothering to wait for answers. He was so much engulfed with fear and so consumed by it that his mind could not function again. Looking straight into his tear-soaked eyes, the other palace guard calmed his nerves down with a few words of assurance. Having heard that, Joseph followed them, but reluctantly, to do exactly what the guards were directed to do for him. Joseph walked out of the prison. When the news finally broke out, it was to the surprise of the other inmates.

"You are not wanted for doing something wrong," the guards solemnly said.

"Take heart dear, for the Pharaoh is in a serious predicament and the whole palace is banking its hope on you."

"Me?" Joseph shot back, even more confused than before.

"*Yes*" the guard answered. "*So, you are coming with us to the palace without any further delay. But first, you are to shave, shower and change into something nice,*" this guard finally said.

The chubby body with which Joseph was thrown into prison had now become a pale shadow of itself. His beautiful skin looked pallid and unwell, and his hair was unkempt. The round socket holding his eyes had almost swallowed them. It seemed to be hiding these eyes from visibility. His bony cheeks protruded and loudly announced a long period of neglect and lack of proper nutrition. There were cracks clearly visible in his thick lips. His whole appearance was out of place and his demeanor spoke volume. Joseph's outward look clearly outlined his frame of mind at the time.

He was brought from the prison to the palace, having changed and dressed up neatly for his meeting with the Pharaoh. This dress was not for a position, but just to look neat in the presence of the king. For the first time in two years, the chief cupbearer set his eyes on the interpreter of dreams. He expressed a mixed feeling of joy and sadness. Joy for seeing the one who interpreted his dream and sadness for not mentioning his name to Pharaoh in time as he promised. Joseph was still trembling from what was happening before his eyes. He had no clue as to what was going on. No one tipped him off as to the purpose for which he was brought to the palace. He was only just told he was wanted by the king, he had no idea what awaited him. So, he trembled visibly. But the kind words from the Pharaoh allayed his fears and his demeanor changed immediately. Yet, despite all that was happening, he was awe-struck for standing in the presence of the most powerful person in the land. Joseph gave the king obeisance. He touched the tip of his golden staff. Pharaoh responded invitingly to the young lad. He did not hesitate at all. Then he cleared his throat. A pin-drop silence invaded every corner of the palace. Then he began to tell Joseph the purpose for which he was summoned to the palace. He spoke thoroughly, and he minced no words.

> *Pharaoh said to Joseph, "I had a dream, and no one can interpret it. But I have heard it said of you that when you hear a dream you can interpret it." "I cannot do it," Joseph replied to Pharaoh, "but God will give Pharaoh the answer he desires" (Genesis 41:15, 16).*

Joseph had been standing since he entered the palace. But when his response seemed to make sense to the Pharaoh, he was ushered to sit on a stool made available for him. He had calmed down now and realized they meant him no harm. With his confidence rising steadily he provided the meaning of the dreams to his audience. The quietness in the hall and all eyes fixed on him, persuaded Joseph to grasp the enormity of the work he was called to do: the interpretation of the dreams. So, he went on to explain, saying;

> *It is just as I said to Pharaoh: God has shown Pharaoh what he is about to do. Seven years of great abundance are coming throughout the land of Egypt, but seven years of famine will follow them. Then all the abundance in Egypt will be forgotten, and the famine will ravage the land. The abundance in the land will not be remembered, because the famine that follows it will be so severe. The reason the dream was given to Pharaoh in two forms is that the matter has been firmly decided by God, and God will do it soon (Genesis 41:28-32).*

For the first time since the Pharaoh rose from his bed that morning, joy leaped into his heart. The whole palace was filled with joy and hope. Everyone knew the meaning of the dream Joseph gave couldn't be far from the truth. As the Pharaoh sat on his throne, he further threw open what should be done to avert the impending hunger that was to plague the nation should they fail to act. Without any hesitation, Joseph suggested to the Pharaoh to look for someone wise and discerning enough to be charged with this tremendous task. That person would collect and store the excess food during the abundant season. The stored food would then be released during the famine. The king slowly nodded approval of Joseph's suggestion. Then he asked, "Who was better fit for such position than Joseph himself?" Turning to his direction,

> *Pharaoh said to Joseph, "Since God has made all this known to you, there is no one so discerning and wise as you. You shall be in charge of my palace, and all my people are to submit to your orders. Only with respect to the throne will I be greater than you" (Genesis 41:39, 40).*

With these words falling from the Pharaoh's lips, Joseph was shocked to the core. He turned and looked at his back as if Pharaoh was talking to someone else. But it was to him. No other person but Joseph. To seal his elevation, Pharaoh called for the LAST COAT of authority he would wear. Then he beckoned Joseph to come toward him. Looking straight into those shocked eyes, Pharaoh made a proclamation. The Bible described the scene thus:

> *So Pharaoh said to Joseph, "I hereby put you in charge of the whole land of Egypt." Then Pharaoh took his signet ring from his finger and put it on Joseph's finger. He dressed him in robes of fine linen and put a gold chain around his neck. He had him ride in a chariot as his second-in-command, and people shouted before him, "Make way!" Thus he put him in charge of the whole land of Egypt. Then Pharaoh said to Joseph, "I am Pharaoh, but without your word no one will lift hand or foot in all Egypt" (Genesis 41:41-44).*

He ordered the palace servants to put the robe on him. Joseph could not assimilate the whole scene. He could not fathom his life changing in a twinkle of an eye; from a wretched prison to a respected position. But it did happen. The invincible mighty hand of God was operating behind the whole episode. He ordered Joseph be paraded through the streets of the city. This was a way of introducing him to the people he would serve. The day closed with the city embracing and accepting Joseph as their new leader; the second in command. When the ceremony had ended, Pharaoh dispersed the small crowd gathered to witness the event.

This event in the palace marked Joseph's journey to the settings for the fulfilment of his dreams. His encounter with problems had paid off; problems that demeaned him. His dignity was thrown into the gutters, his integrity was questioned and his reputation dented with that false accusation. However, at the end of the day, it opened another chapter in his life; this time not as a slave or a servant, but an occupant of a prominent position. The kind of position where he would interact with dignified people of his caliber in the country. It is said, "When there is crack in a wall all kinds of insect throng in there." It implies that, when you fall victim to an unfortunate situation, anyone could exercise the guts to advice you. Some will go to the extent of casting aspersions on your person and decisions, forgetting the fact that, it might be God working to shape a destiny. Joseph's predicament placed him at the mercy of those who were not supposed to treat him as such, but did. But in all these occurrences, Joseph did not sin against

God. In fact, in the whole narrative, it was frequently stated that the Lord was with him.

Chapter Five

MY THOUGHT

"To the person who pleases him, God gives wisdom, knowledge and happiness, but to the sinner he gives the task of gathering and storing up wealth to hand it over to the one who pleases God...." (Ecclesiastes 2:26).

That very night when Joseph was elevated to that high office, and when all was said and done, he might have sat all by himself in a secluded place. In this hallowed place as he sat quietly, I believe, he would be reflecting upon the traumas he experienced in the past thirteen years. These experiences might be flooding his mind, and be playing back and forth. Joseph might have made attempts to piece these experiences together but they could not stick, they could not hold. And so, with a noisy sound, he sighed a big relief, without considering the extent to which this noise would go. *"These occurrences were despicable, they were horrible,"* he might have silently said to himself. Then his eyes had accumulated tears as he remembered some of these past events. Those moments of sorrow and joy, pain and gain, trial and triumph, rejection and acceptance, despair and faith.

Moments that would forever be ingrained on his mind. *"But through it all I chose to trust in the God of my fathers and I prevailed,"* he might have soliloquized, releasing him from the deep thought that had taken hold of him. Joseph pondered the cruelty and fury his brothers spewed, the brutal manhandling they displayed and the foul words they churned when he pleaded for his life. His effort to persuade the Ishmaelite buyers to desist from buying him when that efforts fell on deaf ears. The false accusation by his master's wife when he was denied the chance to present his side of the story. And the cupbearer's inability to make do with his promise when he solemnly swore he would not forget Joseph's kind gesture. All these scenarios caused his body to tremble as he deeply and consciously deliberated them. *"The arm of flesh cannot and must not be depended upon wholly apart from God,"* Joseph advised from his experience, while he correspondingly shook his head. In course of his journey, the successive disappointments and the extreme distress conspired to obscure his view of God, of human nature and of himself. But, however it went, the adversities he faced and the advances he made convinced him to see the whole picture God was painting. That he was being prepared for a position he would occupy. Joseph got the opportunity to learn the techniques of leadership through all these events. He also learned the essence of relationships; the importance of every human being and their contributions to our lives. That everyone of us, at some point in our lives, would need someone's assistance. That it should be required of us therefore, to treat others with respect and dignity. And that was exactly what he did when he met the officials from the palace in the prison. If Joseph had not treated the cupbearer with respect, despite the interpretation, when it was time for him to reciprocate, he would have pretended he didn't recollect what Joseph did.

Friend, critically analyzing Joseph's story, a story he would have wished it never happened, it can be accepted easily and unequivocally as pathetic, profound and painful. It could also be admitted as excruciating, exhausting and ethereal. It is a story in which Joseph defied the poor conspiracy of time and survived the inevitable test of his faith. This is a story enough time is seriously needed to dissect its content and, its nugget carefully exhumed to meet life's demands head on. For this story's timeless lessons cannot be exhausted, its faultless encouragement cannot be curbed and its limitless inspiration cannot be measured. Lessons that, there are reasons for whatever we might be going through. That, the fact that things are delaying does not mean we are going to be denied that which we are seeking from God. That whatever the Lord had said concerning us shall surely come to pass. Encouragement that, something good will surely come at the end of all we might be going through.

That, despite the words folks might throw at us, we are going to succeed. Inspiration that, we must keep moving on no matter the magnitude of adversities or the opposition. That the opposition is there to teach us lessons. That we should not make any attempt to quit. That we should hold on to that which we have purposed in our lives to achieve. James, writing to the saints scattered abroad, concluded encouragingly thus;

> *Blessed is the one who perseveres under trial because, having stood the test, that person will receive the crown of life that the Lord has promised to those who love him (James 1:12).*

Many times, Joseph might have harshly blamed himself for his predicament, and might have thought of quitting. *"If only I had not told anyone of my dreams,"* he would have suggested. *"This whole drama wouldn't have even started and sleeping dogs would have just be lying,"* he might have concluded. But it did happen. The prison - the last place he ever thought would be his abode - had indeed become his residence. The prison environment had a devastating effect on the chap. Joseph's sense of worth was distorted and impaired by the filter of misery he suffered along the way. His posture indicated all the regret. It was clear and visible when he chatted with the cupbearer. His mind played games with him; he thought he could curry favor with him. So, he expressed his frustrations to him.

> *But when all goes well with you, remember me and show me kindness; mention me to Pharaoh and get me out of this prison. I was forcibly carried off from the land of the Hebrews, and even here I have done nothing to deserve being put in a dungeon" (Genesis 40:14, 15).*

Joseph knew so well the cupbearer was in his last days of prison life. He was going back to take his cherished position as that faithful server. Joseph's faith had been so much stretched at this point that he wanted to rely on the arm of flesh. He thought that man could deliver him from his predicament. Once a very bubbling lad, Joseph had become a feeble image of vulnerability and fragility. He was at the lowest point of his life. His back was against the wall and the little hope left in him was draining gradually. He could not hope anymore. Everything around him seemed to be sending messages of failure. But then Joseph paused and considered the might and the power of God. He cast his mind back to those words of God his father taught them whenever they sat around that little burning fire. The stories of the powerful miracles He performed against their enemies. And he drew strength and resilience from them during those turbulent times. It encouraged him, to say the least, for some time. Then when the fullness of time had come for God's intentions - Joseph's presence and position in the palace - to manifest, God orchestrated circumstances that would result in its fulfillment. He did not solicit any help from Joseph, yet God did it to his astonishment. "The greatest test of faith is when you don't get what you want but still you are able to say, 'Thank you Lord'" Pastor John Hagee aptly said.

Elijah expressed similar sentiments. At a point he became fearful. When he spectacularly defeated the prophets of Baal, wicked Jezebel threatened his life. He took to his heels. He found himself frustrated, confused and agitated. The faith this great man of God possessed drained as fast as it could possibly be imagined. His faith was put on the line and he miserably could not stand a minute. Prevailing circumstances compelled Elijah to act in that manner. He was subdued by fear and overtaken by discouragement, culminating in this bizarre behavior. You could act in the same manner should you be overwhelmed by any expected eventuality. The Bible describes it that,

> *Elijah was afraid and ran for his life. When he came to Beersheba in Judah, he left his servant there, while he himself went a day's journey into the wilderness. He came to a broom bush, sat down under it and prayed that he might die. "I have had enough, Lord," he said. "Take my life; I am no better than my ancestors" (1 Kings 19:3, 4).*

David was not excluded from this exclusive club of doubters. When David and his men returned to Ziglak, where they left their wives and children, the Amalekites invaded the city. The raiders burned down the city and took away their wives and children as captives. This mighty warrior was so shocked that he and his fighters "wept aloud until they had no strength left to weep" (1 Samuel 30:4). It was at this juncture that David raised his voice, crying to the "Lord, do not forsake me; do not be far from me, my God. Come quickly to help me, my Lord and my Savior" (Psalm 38:21, 22).

John the Baptist was also caught up in this same web; in a situation he never expected was coming. A situation that exposed the vulnerability of this mighty man of God when he was falsely accused and hurriedly sent to the dungeon. This was the man who introduced the Messiah to the needing world. The man who confessed in the presence of his disciples that they should "…Look, the Lamb of God, who takes away the sin of the world!" (John 1:29). The One whose sandals he was not fit to untie. Afterwards, John finding himself in this unbearable circumstance, "…sent his disciples to ask him, 'Are you the one who is to come, or should we expect someone else?'" (Matthew 11:2, 3).

The atrocities of Cavalry cross were fast approaching. The enormity of the punishment to be visited upon Him, on our behalf, was taking its toll. The betrayal to be instigated by a close ally even further exacerbated His anxiety. So,

Jesus, having deemed it fit and appropriate, withdrew a little further and talked to the Father. In this sequestered place, He poured His heart out saying;

> *"Father, if you are willing, take this cup from me; yet not my will, but yours be done." An angel from heaven appeared to him and strengthened him. And being in anguish, he prayed more earnestly, and his sweat was like drops of blood falling to the ground (Luke 22:42-44).*

In fact, irrespective of how long we have been walking with the Lord, or how matured we might have convinced ourselves to be, we would be gripped with and crippled by fear at a certain time. We could be incapacitated by this fear and could take full control over every facet of our lives. It could take the better part of one's existence. We could then be imprisoned by chronophobia (the irrational fear of the future and of passage of time). During this period, life would seem meaningless and things that are attractive would look otherwise. Reclusion then, could be thought as the best option, the only way out. If care is not taken, one's vibrant life could degenerate into a state with the absence of joy and delight. But the truth is that, when it happens in this manner, be aware that it is just an expression of your humanity and its frailty. In fact, it is not sinful, if at a time you fell victim to such circumstances. Take a cue from these folks, for the greatest danger is when one denies the existence of God, of Jesus Christ and of the Holy Spirit. It would then result in apostasy. Most heroes of the Bible who fell victim to such situations queried God. And these queries revealed their apprehension so sadly. This attitude of doubting had been a human malady since time immemorial.

On some occasions, we may find ourselves in such conditions. Where and when everyone seems to be succeeding, we fail. While others are talking of things they will do in the future, we are left without contributing a word because we had never achieved anything meaningful with our plans before. Failure had become an albatross hanging around our necks. You might be in a state now where you cannot dream anymore, you cannot exercise your faith anymore. But I want you to know that every failure is a learning process. *"Every setback is a setup for a comeback,"* as most folks are fond of saying. The giving of a new coat to Joseph in course of his journey to the palace marked a new beginning, but every stripping of same presented him with a teachable moment.

"There is always light at the end of the tunnel," it is usually said. And it is true.

- But why don't we see this light at the onset of life?
- Why does life seem unbearable at the beginning and filled with disappointments going forward?

- Why does the future seem to look bleak at the initial stages? Why?

These are hard questions we might be compelled to ask should we find ourselves in any awkward situation. And they are genuine. But the answer is simple. It is because the tunnel is not straight, but crooked. If the tunnel had been straight, we will just run at a terrific speed towards the light, skipping the very lessons we are supposed to learn along the tunnel. So, God, in His infinite wisdom, made it crooked so that at the turn of every corner we will pause and navigate it slowly. That is just the way it is with life, my dear friends. If whatever we touch should turn to 'gold,' there would not be any teachable moment for us to acquire wisdom. He does not rejoice when we are in pains but sometimes, He allows them to come for our sakes. It is He who, on some occasions, permits failures and disappointments to intrude upon our lives. He uses them as opportunities to teach us. God shows His greatness in our shortcomings and failures. In fact, God considers "that our present sufferings are not worth comparing with the glory that will be revealed in us" (Romans 8:18). This is how the Hebrews' letter writer articulated it to its recipients. It reads thus, "No discipline seems pleasant at the time, but painful. Later on, however, it produces a harvest of righteousness and peace for those who have been trained by it" (Hebrews 12:11).

You might be going through some circumstances at this moment. Life had not been treating you fairly these days. Every attempt to emerge and reinvent yourself is met by failure, one after another. Therefore, your confidence is draining, your courage is waning and your commitment is slipping away by the day. Your once-organized life had scattered, and the pieces are there to prove your present predicament. Life had become so tough that you have become a laughing stock among your peers. And they ridicule and humiliate you because you are still struggling to make your mark on the scene. They take your words out of context, or simply put, add what you have not said and run away with it. Those aspirations, once held so dear to your heart, are on the chopping block. Your dreams are dead and the gifted talent is now corroded. Every effort to resuscitate these dead dreams and talent once so admired and cherished is not materializing. Your effort cannot match the daily pressure pushing against you. The many sleepless nights and the accompanying sweat you experience, even on cold days, cannot be denied. Your friends, and foes alike, are using your situation as the parameter to define your destiny. No one seems to understand your feelings, and your words are not sufficient to explain. For that matter, you have decided to keep silent. And they interpret this silence as weakness or effortlessness or you, not being serious in life. You are so overwhelmed by the prevailing circumstances that you are pushed to the verge of giving up your hopes and dreams. You want to throw in the towel. May I plead with you to hang on, for in no time, God will come through with you. Take time to learn every day that which He wants you to know. He is doing something in your life you have no idea of. For I am so "... confident of this, that he who began a good work in you will carry it on to completion until the day of Christ Jesus" (Philippians 1:6). One wise person once said, *"The greatest mistake we make in life is not the mistake we made, but the refusal to learn from the mistake is rather, the greatest mistake."* Bear in mind that, without a trial, there is no triumph; without a mess, there is no message and without a cross, there is no crown. You are a winner! What words of wisdom do you have if you had not been in these kinds of circumstances before? God is going to use you personally and the experiences you acquire to change someone's circumstances of similar magnitude. David endured similar predicament in life, and said so well afterwards;

> *Even though I walk through the valley of the shadow of death, I will fear no evil, for you are with me; your rod and your staff, they comfort me. You prepare a table before me in the presence of my enemies. You anoint my head with oil; my cup overflows (Psalm 23:4, 5).*

The table will be prepared before you only when you come out of the valley. These heroic men, and many others, exhibited bouts of fear and doubt in their walk with God. But with all their fears and doubts, they never wavered in their faith in Him. They stayed under God's banner and walked with Him to the best of their faith and ability. Ponder this quote since you're coming to the end this book. A cousin friend of mine sent it to me through the social media a few months ago. Its author was not identified. Yet, it shouldn't be denied sharing, as a way of encouraging you.

Never get disappointed when things happened beyond expectations. Remember that the greatest glory in life is rising when you fall. Be strong and have faith. Sometimes life doesn't give what you want, not because you don't deserve it, but because you deserve better. No matter how many times you break down, there should be a little voice inside you that says, NO, you're not done yet! Be strong, keep hope alive (Anonymous).

My Thoughts

Conclusion

"But God chose the foolish things of the world to shame the wise; God chose the weak things of the world to shame the strong. God chose the lowly things of this world and the despised things - and the things that are not - to nullify the things that are, so that no one may boast before him" (1 Corinthians 1:27-29).

Though life has its own sets of rules, sometimes these rules do not play the way they are expected or supposed to. The disappointments we face in life, in turn, increase the frustration that comes with it. Where one person succeeds, another fails, though they follow the same procedures. It is so baffling beyond one's comprehension. It is for this reason life is said to be complex and complicated at the same time. That is also why the future is said to be unknown. But, irrespective of the circumstances one might go through or experience, if one would learn to remain sturdy under the banner of God, the outcome shall be fulfilling. David made this sacred and secured declaration that,

> *The Lord makes firm the steps of the one who delights in him; though he may stumble, he will not fall, for the Lord upholds him with his hand. I was young and now I am old, yet I have never seen the righteous forsaken or their children begging bread (Psalm 37:23-25).*

Conclusion

While we are all created by God, His purposes for us; for our being in this world, vary from person to person. And for Joseph too, his purpose was also different. In his dreams, God revealed his destiny but not the process through which he would achieve it. Though he was denied the knowledge of this process, it did not prevent him from going through those tough situations. It is this kind of denial that diminishes our patience and escalates our anxiety. In fact, just as a destination determines the direction one should take to get there, so it is with our destiny. What one is destined to be will determine the kind of conditions one must endure. It is out of these enduring circumstances our flaws are exposed and dealt with. Also, our strength is harnessed and well nurtured to maturity. God knew all the obstacles Joseph would have to overcome, all the objections he would have to face and all the oppositions he would have to endure, yet He gave him the dreams. Yet He allowed him to reveal the dreams to the family. Why didn't God prevent all these things, but allowed them? The reason is simple: it is the importance God attached to his destiny. We often decry the trials and the tests but God's interest is in the outcome and our contribution to fulfill His plans and purposes. While we complain bitterly about the process, God explains beautifully about the product. God does not care how difficult the process might be; His interest is in the product. And you are a product He is working on. On that note, Apostle Paul always reminds us to "... know that in all things God works for the good of those who love him, who have been called according to his purpose" (Romans 8:28).

The medical doctor, the pharmacist, the nurse and the driver, all work in the hospital to make it function well. Each morning, they would proudly wear their badges - made from the same material and beautifully decorated with the same colors - across their breasts as they make their way to the hospital. It is through the combined efforts of these professionals that the hospital runs effectively and successfully to discharge its duties to patients at the end of the day. Happily, they contribute in their various capacities to help achieve the purposes for which the hospital is built. Though these hospital workers share many things in common, certainly there is one thing that differentiates one from the other. This difference distinguishes them from each person with regards to their career output, accountability and work demand and that difference is their training. When it comes to the training for their various specialties, they do not spend the same number of days, months and years in school. Though they might probably start their various courses the same day, month or even the same year, it is the required demand of their careers that would then determine the number of years needed to prepare. That is just the way God prepares the believer. The various calling upon our lives would determine what the Lord would have to take us through. That was why Joseph had to pass through those unfortunate circumstances before rising to this position in Egypt. The response to your cry to the Lord for your circumstances might be delayed in coming, or seemed to be denied. Know one thing, it is the magnitude of the task for which you are called, that would decide your course of training. Something big for you is in the offing. Therefore,

> *Trust in the Lord with all your heart and lean not on your own understanding; in all your ways acknowledge him, and he will make your paths straight. Do not be wise in your own eyes; fear the Lord and shun evil (Proverbs 3:5-7).*

On the day when all the animals were herded into the ark Noah built, there were swift animals, like the antelope, which would gallop a few minutes and get into the ark. At the same time, there were some that were slow, like the tortoise, yet they all entered the ark before it was closed. It has been long in manifesting that which you aspired to achieve. Every Monday, you get a new job or something, hoping that it would last permanently, but to be lost the next Friday. It has gone on like this for some time now. There is that thing you have been asking from God that is coming your way soon. It will not only be PERMANENT, but PROMINENT. Joseph would have to take off three coats to make way for the last: the BEST and the MOST

BEAUTIFUL. Every coat he wore, and then taken off without his consent, equipped him with the experience needed to wear the very last one. It had not been easy for Joseph; the frustration, the anxiety and the confusion. But at the end of the day, his abiding spirit and enduring strength kept him through these turbulent times. The constant change in your situations - from bad to worse - is to equip you also with experience for that thing you are seeking from God permanently. The success story of others should not, by any means, discourage you at all. Let it inspire you to achieve yours. For on that fateful Friday night when all dust had settled and calm had returned to the city, the dark world began to jubilate over the death of our Lord Jesus Christ. Satan rallied his cohorts to celebrate their 'victory' over their archenemy. But little did he know his move would rather bring the end of his grip on mankind. That it was the beginning of the hope promised man long ago in the garden. That it was the new dawn of freedom for human race through the blood shed on Calvary's mountain. That Sunday morning was speedily coming when the grave would not hold Him captive anymore. The apostle Matthew captured it this way;

> The angel said to the women, "Do not be afraid, for I know that you are looking for Jesus, who was crucified. He is not here; he has risen, just as he said. Come and see the place where he lay. Then go quickly and tell his disciples: 'He has risen from the dead and is going ahead of you into Galilee.

> *There you will see him.' Now I have told you"* (Matthew 28:5-7).

From Joseph's journey and his ascension to the position, we can easily conclude that sometimes God allows disappointment, confusion, discouragement, hopelessness, helplessness, tough times and unimagined predicaments to come our ways. He does this by interfering with our regular routines in different and diverse ways since life has its funny way of dealing with us. He does this so He can work on us. Life is full of adversities. Joseph was no exception, and we are neither going to be also. Therefore, Joseph's resilience in the face of adversities should inspire us to keep on trying a little further. He faultlessly embraced life's setbacks and genuinely wove his personal life through them to the fullest. His beatific expression of joy, fragile as a perfect child's, when he ascended that high office should be a source of encouragement to anyone going through tough times. That it shall be well; that it shall come to an end. Something good is about to fall on you. You are about to celebrate your breakthrough; a breakthrough Satan had stifled for a long time. The writer of Ecclesiastes had been where you are now. From this experience he admonished that,

> *The race is not to the swift or the battle to the strong, nor does food come to the wise or wealth to the brilliant or favor*

to the learned; but time and chance happen to them all (Ecclesiastes 9:11).

Take heart as this verse encourages you in your walk with God. May the Lord richly bless you in all your attempts to achieve something meaningful for yourself.

COMPARE AND CONTRAST THE COATS

Wearing the First three coats	*Wearing the Last Coat (Gen. 41)*
Others were in charge	*Joseph was in charge (41:41)*
Ordinary people gave him the coats	*A King gave him the coat (v.42)*
Walked before men	*Men walked before him (v.43a)*
Temporal positions	*Permanent position (v. 43b)*
Joseph was given orders	*Joseph gave orders (v. 44)*
Name maintained	*Name changed (v. 45)*
Joseph served	*Joseph was served (v.46-49)*

Conclusion

WATCH OUT

for

DESTINY

JOSEPH'S DREAMS ARE FULFILLED
A SEQUEL TO

'THE LAST COAT'

NOTE TO THE READER

Joseph's arrival in the palace is not the fulfilment of his dreams. No, it is not the ultimate. It is rather the setting up of the stage for the dreams to be ultimately fulfilled, hence a sequel. The next book, "DESTINY," therefore comes as the sequel. This book will explore vividly Joseph's roadmap to the destiny God carved and revealed to him about thirteen years earlier. His brothers thought they could prevent it from being fulfilled. Joseph's entire story and the lessons embedded it would not be fully grasped if both books are not read. It would do you a great disservice if you failed to grab both copies. Look forward to the publishing of the sequel in no distant a time with the same anxiety you would other things you so much desire. Thank you.

Author